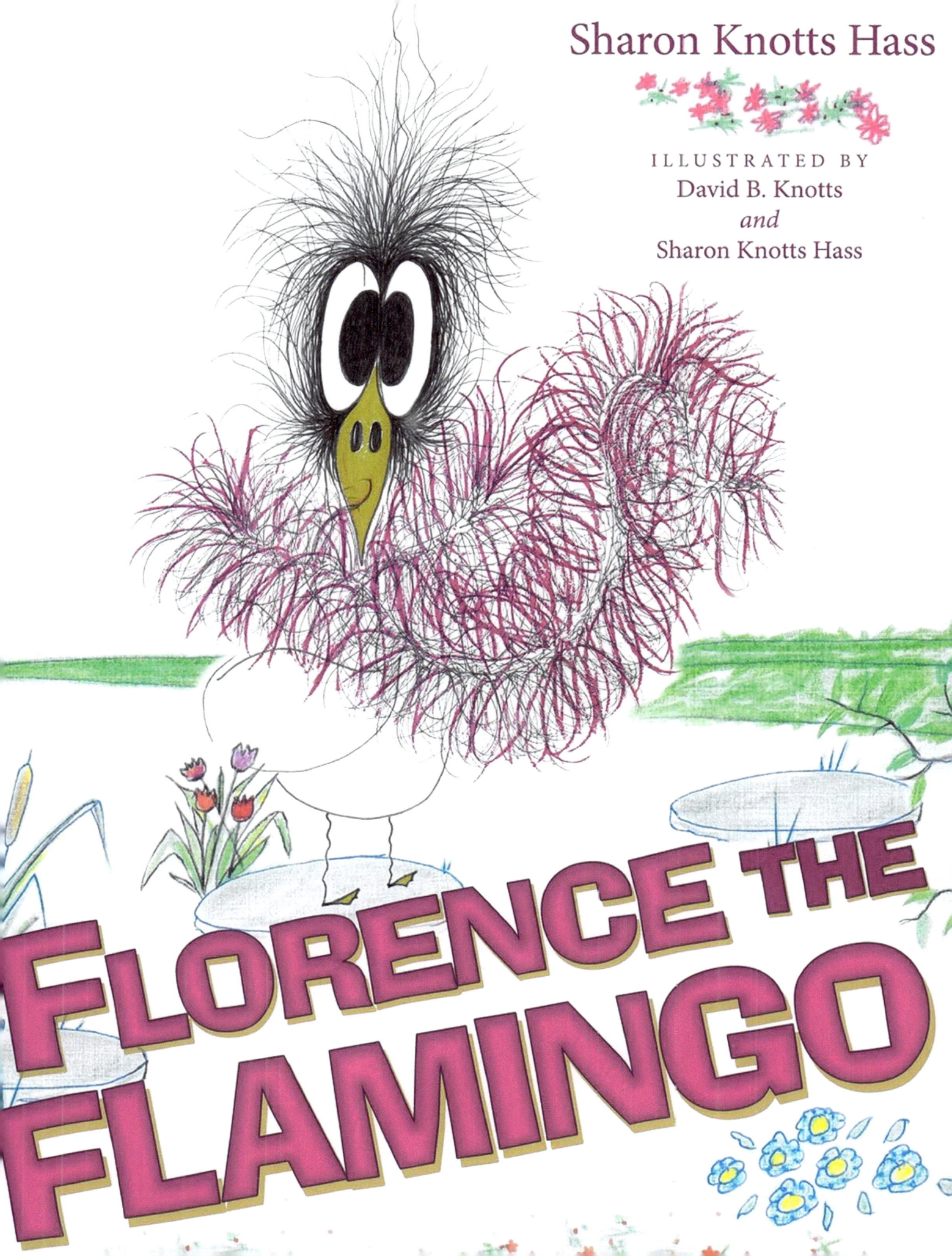

Sharon Knotts Hass

ILLUSTRATED BY
David B. Knotts
and
Sharon Knotts Hass

FLORENCE THE FLAMINGO

FLORENCE THE FLAMINGO

Sharon Knotts Hass

ILLUSTRATED BY
David B. Knotts
and
Sharon Knotts Hass

WORKBOOK PRESS LLC
187 E Warm Springs Rd,
Suite B285, Las Vegas, NV 89119, USA

Website: https://workbookpress.com/
Hotline: 1-888-818-4856
Email: admin@workbookpress.com

Ordering Information:
Quantity sales. Special discounts are available on quantity purchases by corporations, associations, and others. For details, contact the publisher at the address above.

Library of Congress Control Number:
ISBN-13:   000-0-00000-000-0 (Paperback Version)
           000-0-00000-000-0 (Digital Version)

REV. DATE: 04/06/2022

Dedicated to the memory of David B. Knotts, my brother, best friend and creator of Florence. He made her for me. ☺

Once upon a time in a far away, enchanted
land, there lived a most interesting,
fluffy, kind and lovely bird.
Her name was Florence the Flamingo.
Here is Florence visiting the Grand Canyon.

She was a very smart and stylish flamingo. She was said to be the most intelligent flamingo ever known. Florence going home after a walk in the park.

You see Florence could not only walk, run
and swim, but she could drive a car, and
she was captain of her own speed boat.
She made her boat go very fast,
but she was careful.

She loved to go for boat rides and watch the blue and white waves splashing behind her. She was amazing on water skis too. She loved the ocean and the beach. Florence was a bit of a show off when it came to showing her water skiing skills.

Florence was always looking for adventure. Driving her fancy car on long, winding roads was a favorite thing to do.

Florence enjoyed watching movies. She often thought about becoming a movie star and living in Hollywood.

Florence was also quite the gardener.

She was very talented.

She grew bright and beautiful flowers.

The flowers and the sunlight made her very happy. She loved to grow red, blue, pink and yellow flowers. Florence often gave them to friends and neighbors, she was very kind.

FLORENCE

IN THE GARDEN

After a relaxing day playing in her garden, Florence would get cleaned up and dress up for tea time. What a way she would end her day.

Oh to have a friend like her.

Florence was a fabulous flamingo.

The End.

Sharon is an animal lover and she loves children and nature's beauty. Growing up in the land of enchantment beneath the most beautiful sunrises and sunsets, led her to recognize and love God's beautiful gift of nature. She has incorporated them in this fun and colorful story about a flashy flamingo named Florence. She has always drawn and painted animals, flowers, mountains, trees etc from a very young age. Her brother David was a big influence on her in the art and humor realm.

Sharon is a big fan of Dr Suess, rhythm and rhyme. She is currently working on two more rhyming children's books.

FLORENCE is a fabulous flamingo. A free-spirited, smart bird with style and many talents, Florence can not only walk, run, and swim, but she can drive a car, and she is captain of her own speed boat.

This flashy flamingo is always looking for adventure, and she finds it water skiing and driving on long, winding roads. Florence loves flowers and gardening and dressing up to go out.

A fun and colorful picture book for children, *Florence the Flamingo* shares a charming story about one bird who loves life and lives it to the fullest.

www.ingramcontent.com/pod-product-compliance
Lightning Source LLC
Chambersburg PA
CBHW041605120626
46551CB00002B/318